help**me**
BECOME™

Becoming *Dependable* &
Overcoming **Breaking Promises**™

REAL
mvpkids®

Pick Your Promises™

SOPHIA DAY®

Written by Kayla Pearson   Illustrated by Timothy Zowada

The Sophia Day® Creative Team-
Kayla Pearson, Timothy Zowada,
Stephanie Strouse, Megan Johnson, Mel Sauder

A **special thank you** to our team of reviewers who graciously
give us feedback, edits and help ensure that our products
remain accurate, applicable and genuinely diverse.

Published and Distributed by MVP Kids Media, LLC -
Mesa, Arizona, USA
Printed by Prosperous Printing Inc. -
Shenzhen, China

Designed by Stephanie Strouse

DOM Aug 2019, Job # 03-012-01

May your childhood be filled with adventure, your days with hope and your learnings with wisdom, and may you continuously grow as an MVP Kid, preparing to lead a responsible, meaningful life.

−SOPHIA DAY

TABLE OF CONTENTS

STORY	PAGE

Aanya's Science Experiment

One morning, Aanya sat next to her friends
Riley and Grace on the way to school.

"Will you jump rope with us at recess today?" asked Riley.

"Sure! That sounds like fun!" said Aanya.

"Promise?" asked Grace.

"Pinky promise!" The girls giggled.

4

When they arrived at school, they saw Mr. Davis had a special science project. Aanya was excited. They were going to grow their own crystals. In order for the crystals to grow, they would have to **sit untouched for a week.**

Mr. Davis asked the class to promise not to touch them until they were ready.

"We promise!"

Aanya said with the rest of the class.

When recess came, some kids asked Aanya to play tag with them.

"That sounds like fun! I'll play!" said Aanya.

"But Aanya, you *promised* you would play with us," said Riley.

"I know, but I want to play tag now." Aanya ran off to play.

Several days passed. Riley and Grace didn't want to play with Aanya at recess.

Aanya didn't understand. Why was changing her mind about playing jump rope such a big deal?

The next day, Aanya didn't want to go out for recess. She asked Mr. Davis if she could stay inside to work on homework. When he wasn't watching, she picked up her crystal to look at it closely. The crystal broke and shattered into little pieces.

DON'T TOUCH

"Mr. Davis, I broke my crystal."

"Oh no! Do you see now why I asked you to promise not to touch it?"

"Yes. I'm sorry."

"You know, crystals are a lot like friendships and the promises you make. When you keep your promises, you create strong friendships because your friends can trust you. When you break your promises, your friends can't rely on what you say," said Mr. Davis.

Aanya thought about how she broke
her promise to Riley and Grace.
She wanted her friends to trust her.
Aanya knew she needed to make things right.

Aanya found Riley and Grace at recess.
"I'm sorry I broke my promise.
May I jump rope with you today?"

Riley and Grace
forgave her.

The three girls
jumped rope together
all recess long.

THINK & TALK ABOUT IT

Aanya's Science Experiment

Discuss the story...

1. What is a promise?

2. Why do you think Aanya broke her promise to Riley and Grace?

3. Why do you think this hurt her friends' feelings?

4. What did Aanya learn about friendships from Mr. Davis?

5. What was Aanya's solution to fixing her friendship?

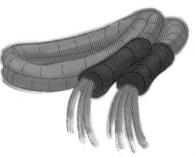

Discuss how to apply the story...

1. Why do you think people make promises?

2. When someone makes a promise to you, do you expect them to keep it?

3. How does it feel when someone keeps a promise?

4. How does it feel when someone breaks a promise?

5. Other than keeping promises, what else can you do to build strong friendships?

FOR PARENTS & MENTORS: *Keeping your word, commitments and promises is a sign that you are a person of integrity, that you value others and that others can trust you. Teaching children about keeping promises begins with your example. Be careful about what promises you make to your children, and always do your best to keep your promises. If something happens where you can't keep your promise, don't pretend it isn't a big deal. Apologize to your child and try to find a way to make it up to them. Not only is keeping promises important for external relationships, but it's also important for personal self-esteem. Children will learn that keeping promises makes their relationships with others stronger as well as helps them feel better about themselves.*

Grow your own crystals at home with Aanya's Homemade Rock Candy Recipe on page 63!

*For additional tips and reference information, visit **www.mvpkids.com**.*

Yong's Talent Show

Yong and his friends were meeting to figure out what they would do for the school talent show.

Yong had an idea. "Let's do a Chinese yo-yo act!"
His friends didn't know how to use a Chinese yo-yo,
so Yong promised to do *all* the work.

He **promised** to pick the music, plan the whole act and teach them how to Chinese yo-yo.

The next weekend the boys got together to practice. However, Yong **hadn't worked** to keep any of his promises.

"I don't think this is such a good idea," said Anthony.

"Yeah, we're never going to have the act ready in time," said Marcus.

Yong promised *again* that he would work on it this week, but his friends didn't believe him. They wanted to give up on the act.

29

At dinner that night, Yong was upset
his friends quit the talent show.
He told his mom about it.

"Yong, you didn't keep your promises. Empty promises are like empty dumplings — sad and disappointing. If you make a promise, you need to do everything you can to keep it. If you don't think you can keep a promise, then you shouldn't promise it."

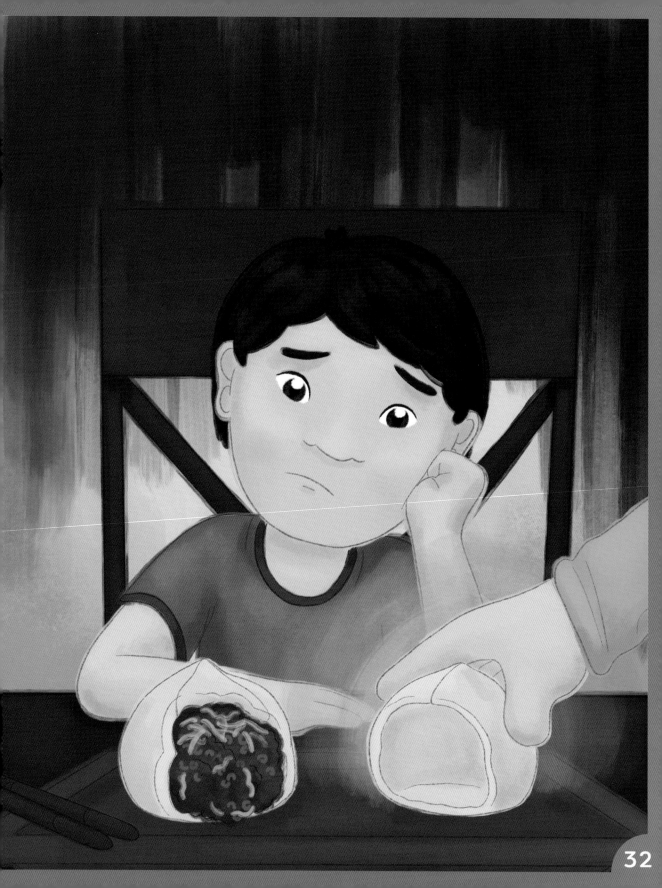

Yong listened to his mom's advice.
He was determined to work hard and
still keep his promise to his friends.

Yong went back to his friends. "I'm sorry for **not keeping my promise at first.** I worked hard to make it up to you. If you will give me a second chance, I think we can have an amazing act for the talent show."

Yong's friends gave him a second chance.
They all worked hard to get ready
for the show.

The night of the talent show came. Yong and his friends performed their act and received a standing ovation! **Yong was glad he kept his promise and didn't disappoint his friends.**

THINK & TALK ABOUT IT

Discuss the story...

1. How do you think Yong's friends felt when Yong first made the promise?

2. How do you think they felt when Yong didn't keep his promise?

3. Why do you think Yong didn't keep his promise?

4. What do you think "empty promises are like empty dumplings" means?

5. How do you think Yong would have felt if he had just given up?

Discuss how to apply the story...

1. What would you do for a talent show?

2. What are some reasons why people break their promises?

3. Describe a time when you broke a promise.

4. What should you do if you break a promise?

5. Why is it important to pick what promises you make?

FOR PARENTS & MENTORS: *One of the biggest obstacles to not keeping promises is making too many commitments and not understanding your own limits. It's easy for people to try to please others and make promises that they think others want to hear. However, it is better to be honest with yourself and others by picking promises you know you can keep. If children are having a hard time keeping promises because they are trying to please others, talk to them about picking their promises wisely. It will please others more for you to be honest with what you can do than to fall through on a promise. Sometimes life happens and unexpected circumstances can arise that cause promises to not be met. If this happens, teach children to go to the person they made a promise to, explain the situation and apologize.*

Frankie's Sleepover

One day, Frankie helped his mom carry the groceries in from the store.

While unpacking the bags, Frankie asked,
"Mom, can I spend the night at Jason's on Friday?"

"What are you guys going to do?"

"Hang out. Play games. Maybe watch a movie."

"I'll have to check with your father, but you have to promise not to watch any scary movies."

"I promise, Mom."

Frankie's mom and dad **trusted him** to keep his promise. He went over to Jason's house and played some video games.

After a while, Jason's brothers came in
and turned off their game.

"We're watching Monster Invasion 4.
If you little kids aren't *too scared*, you
can watch it with us big kids."

"We're not too scared. We'll watch it!"
said Jason.

Frankie thought about the promise he made to his mom. He didn't want to **break his promise,** but he didn't want the others **to make fun of him.**

Frankie had an idea. "Who wants to go out and play capture the flag in the dark?"
He hoped this would let him keep his promise without looking like he was afraid.

Frankie's friends loved his idea!

They grabbed their flashlights and went outside.
Jason's brothers teased them as they left, but
Frankie didn't care. He was glad his friends didn't
want to watch the movie either.

Frankie and his friends split into two teams, hid the flags and began the game. Frankie had a blast!

This is way better *than watching some scary movie,* he thought.

When the game was over, they went back inside the house. The scary movie was over, and Jason's brothers looked terrified. This made Frankie even more **thankful** he didn't watch it.

The next morning, Frankie went home and told his mom about how much fun he had. He even told her about how he kept his promise. This made her happy.

"I'm so glad I can depend on you to keep your promises."

THINK & TALK ABOUT IT

Frankie's Sleepover

Discuss the story...

1. Why do you think Frankie's mom did not want him to watch scary movies?

2. What do you think the word "trust" means?

3. Do you think Frankie's friends were glad Frankie suggested going outside?

4. How do you think Frankie's parents would have felt if Frankie had broken his promise?

5. What do you think would have happened if Frankie would have broken his promise?

Discuss how to apply the story...

1. Who are people you trust in your life?

2. Who do you think can trust you?

3. What are some things your parents depend on you to do?

4. Can your parents depend on you to keep your promises when they aren't around you?

5. If you were in Frankie's situation, what would you have done?

FOR PARENTS & MENTORS: *Relationships are built on trust, the belief that you can rely on someone for something. Trust is built by two people and goes both ways between parent-child and child-parent. It is just as important for you to be able to trust your child as it is for your child to be able to trust you. Build trust with children by creating a safe environment at home where children feel their needs are met. Empathize with children so they feel like they can trust you with their emotions as well. As children get older, it is natural for them to want more independence that requires more trust. Allow children to earn your trust by giving them slightly more responsibility. If a promise or your trust is broken, empathize with children, but also show them that there are consequences until trust can be rebuilt.*

*For additional tips and reference information, visit **www.mvpkids.com**.*

Meet the

mvpkids®

featured in

Pick Your Promises™

with their families

AANYA PATEL

YONG CHEN

MRS. LI CHEN
"Mom"

FRANKIE RUSSO

EZEKIEL JORDAN

MRS. CLAUDIA
RUSSO
"Mom"

Aanya's Homemade Rock Candy Recipe

Important Safety Note: *This recipe contains steps that may be dangerous and should be carried out under responsible adult supervision. In particular, this recipe involves the use of a stove, boiling water and potentially hot containers and is inherently dangerous for children. The author and publisher expressly disclaim responsibility for any injury or damages that result from engaging in the exercise contained herein.*

MATERIALS NEEDED:

2 wood skewers

4 clothes pins

2 small jars *(safe for hot water)*

2 cups water

3.5 cups sugar

Food coloring

PREPARATION:

• The day before you want to make your crystals, prepare your wood skewers by getting them wet and completely covering them with sugar.

• Sit them aside to dry over night.

• Clean the glass jars thoroughly with hot water.

DIRECTIONS:

1. Once your skewers that are covered in sugar are dry, hang them from the top of the glass jars using clothespins so that they are hanging one inch from the bottom of the jar.

2. Have an adult boil two cups of water in a pot on the stove. *(Do NOT use a microwave to boil water.)*

3. Add the sugar into the pot one cup at a time, stirring and letting each cup dissolve in the water before adding another cup of sugar. Continue until all 3.5 cups of sugar have dissolved.

4. Have an adult remove the pot from the stove, and let it sit for about 10 minutes. Then, have an adult pour the hot sugar water into your two clean jars that are safe for hot water. *(Use oven mitts to handle hot objects.)*

5. Add a couple drops of food coloring and gently stir. Then, let the jar sit for 3-5 days as the crystals begin to form. Do not touch or move the jar or skewer in any way during this time.

6. After 3-5 days, carefully remove the skewers with the crystal formations, and allow them to dry.

Grow up with our **mvp**kids®

CELEBRATE!™
Board Books
Ages 0-6

Our **CELEBRATE™** board books for toddlers and preschoolers focus on social, emotional, educational and physical needs. Helpful Teaching Tips are included in each book to equip parents to guide their children deeper into the subject of each book.

Celebrate!™
Paperbacks
Ages 4-8

Our **Celebrate!™** paperback books for Pre-K to Grade 2 focus on social and emotional learning. Helpful Teaching Tips are included in each book to equip mentors and parents. Also available are expertly written, related SEL curriculum and interactive e-book apps.

help**me**
UNDERSTAND™
Elementary
Ages 6-12

Our **Help Me Understand™** series for elementary readers shares the stories of our MVP Kids® learning to understand and manage specific emotions. Readers will gain tools to take responsibility for their own emotions and develop healthy relationships.

Help your children grow in character by collecting the entire **Help Me Become™** series!

*Our **Help Me Become™** series for early elementary readers tells three short stories in each book of our MVP Kids® inspiring character growth. Each story concludes with a discussion guide to help the child process the story and apply the concepts.*

*Learn about our **Social and Emotional Learning Curriculum**,
puppets and more at **www.mvpkidsED.com**.*

*To view our full list of products, visit **www.mvpkids.com**.*

YONG CHEN

LEO RUSSO

FRANKIE RUSSO

JULIA ROJAS

GABBY GONZÁLEZ

ANNIE JAMES

AANYA PATEL

BLAKE JAMES

SARAH COHEN-GOLDSTEIN